Pink Series
Language Work Book

Age 4+

Ogabidu Emmanuel

Ogabidu Emmanuel

Dedication

This book is dedicated to God Almighty and wife

TEACHER'S GUIDE

This book is a workbook that children are expected to work with.

The book should be used as a way of re-inforcing the basic teaching of sound.

Before using this workbook ensure that the concept has been taught using relevant Montessori materials like:

1. The sandpaper letter
2. Large Moveable Alphabets(LMA) and Small Moveable Alphabet (SMA)
3. Three period lesson
   Naming: This is ....
   Association/recognition: Show me ....
   Recall: What is this ....

This book contains all the exercises for the pink scheme. Teachers should endeavour to plan activities that will aid children's understanding of sight words as contained in this workbook.

Ensure children are expose to concrete materials such as the LMA and SMA, the object boxes and picture cards.

Table of Contents

Review of Last Term's Work

Date:_____Title:_____

Letters of the Alphabet

Small letters

a b c d e f g h i j k l m n
o p q r s t u v w x y z

Capital Letters

A B C D E F G H I J K L M
N O P Q R S T U V W X Y Z

Capital Letters and Small Letters

Aa Bb Cc Dd Ee Ff Gg Hh Ii Jj
Kk Ll Mm Nn Oo Pp Qq Rr Ss Tt
Uu Vv Ww Xx Yy Zz

Write small letters a-z

_____

_____

_____

_____

_____

Letters of the Alphabet

Write capital letters A-Z

_____
....
_____
_____
....
_____
_____
....

Write the missing letters

A__   __b   __c   D__   __e   F__   __g   H__

I__   __j   K__   __l   M__   N__   __o   __p

Q__   __r   S__   __t   U__   __v   W__   __x

__y   Z__

Write capital and small letters Aa-Zz

_____
....
_____
_____
....
_____
_____
....
_____

Date:_____Title:_____

Sounds and object chart a-z

 a

 b

 c

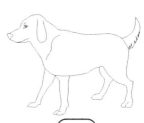 d

 e

 f

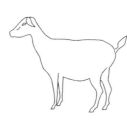 g

 h

 i

 j

 k

 l

 m

 n

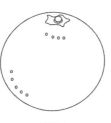 o

p

Date:_____Title:_____

Sounds and object chart a-z

q

r

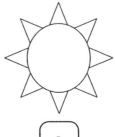
s

t

u

v

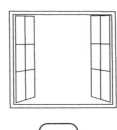
w

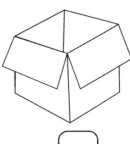
x

y

z

Date:_____Title:_____

Say the name of each object and write the beginning sound.

Date:_____Title:_____

Say the name of each object and write the beginning sound.

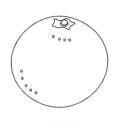 ☐ 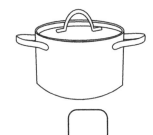 ☐  ☐  ☐

 ☐  ☐  ☐  ☐

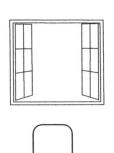 ☐ 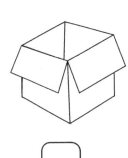 ☐  ☐  ☐

Date:_____ Title:_____

Match each object to the correct sound.

   p      k

     d      c

   l      o

   b      g

   m   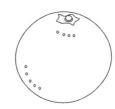   l

   e   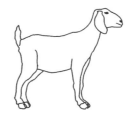   h

Date:_____Title:_____

Match each sound to the correct object.

f	
i	
q	
t	
o	
a	

w	
r	
v	
z	
n	
j	

Vowels and Consonants

Vowels

a b c d e f g h i j k l m n
o p q r s t u v w x y z

Vowels are: Aa Ee Ii Oo Uu

Circle the vowels write them in the box.

a b c d e f g h i j k l m n

o p q r s t u v w x y z

Circle all the vowels

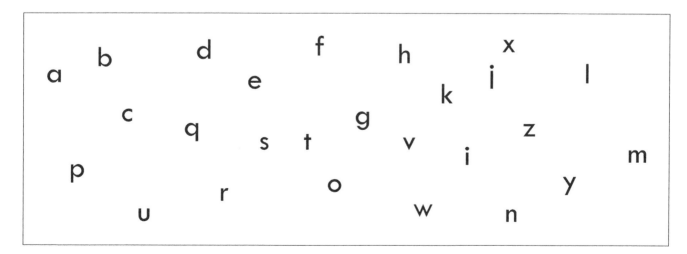

Vowels are special letters. We call them by their letter name.

Consonants

a b c d e f g h i j k l m n
o p q r s t u v w x y z

Consonants are: Bb Cc Dd Ff Gg Hh

Jj Kk Ll Mm Nn Pp Qq Rr Ss Tt
Vv Ww Xx Yy Zz

Circle all the consonants

a b c d e f g h i j k l m n

o p q r s t u v w x y z

Write all the consonant from b - z

_____
....
_____
_____
....
_____
_____
....
_____

Date:_____Title:_____

Two Letter Words

a + t =   _____

a + n =   _____

a + m =   _____

a + s =   _____

i + n =   _____

i + t =   _____

i + f =   _____

i + s =   _____

o + f =   _____

o + n =   _____

Date:_____Title:_____

Two Letter Words

at

as

am

in

if

on

go

(12)

Date:_____Title:_____

Underline the beginning sound and write it out.

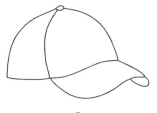 <u>c</u> a p c

 peg

 b a g

 apple

 l o g

 sun

 h e n

 fish

 r a bbit

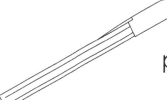 pen

 w e b

 cot

Date:_____ Title:_____

Write the beginning sound of each object.

  | b | 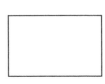 [ ]

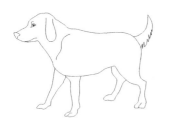 [ ]    [ ]

 [ ]    [ ]

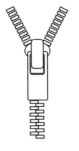 [ ]   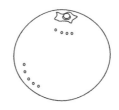 [ ]

 [ ]   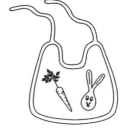 [ ]

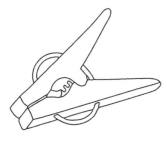 [ ]    [ ]

Date:_____ Title:_____

Circle the middle sounds.

 c (a) p

 h a t

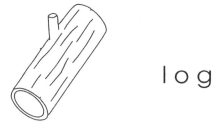 l o g

 w e b

 b a g

 h e n

 lid

 bed

 sun

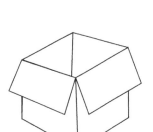 mop

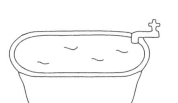 fox

tub

15

Date:_____ Title:_____

Say the name of each object and write the middle sound.

b<u>e</u>d

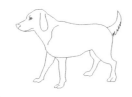

d_g

b_t

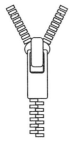

z_p

l_g

p_g

Date:_____Title:_____

Write the middle sounds.

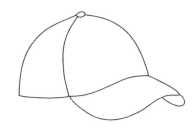

c___p

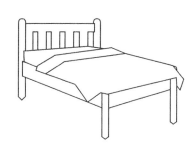

b___d

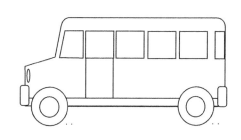

b___s

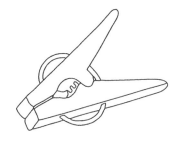

z___p

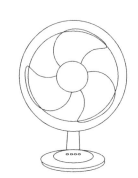

f___n

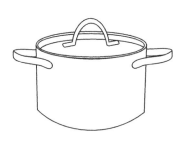

p___t

b___g

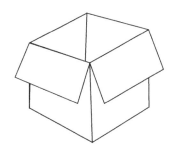

b___x

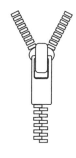

z___p

17

Box 1

Short Vowel 'a'

18

Date:_____Title:_____

Touch and say the name of each object and write the beginning sound.

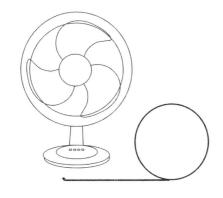

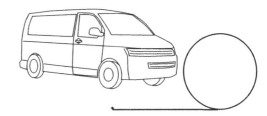

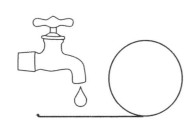

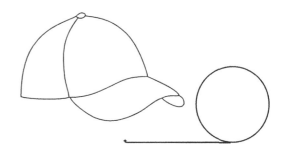

19

Date:_____Title:_____

Sound, blend and write

v + a + n = _____

f + a + n = _____

c + a + t = _____

t + a + p = _____

c + a + p = _____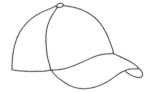

b + a + g = _____

20

Date:_____Title:_____

Match the picture with the correct word

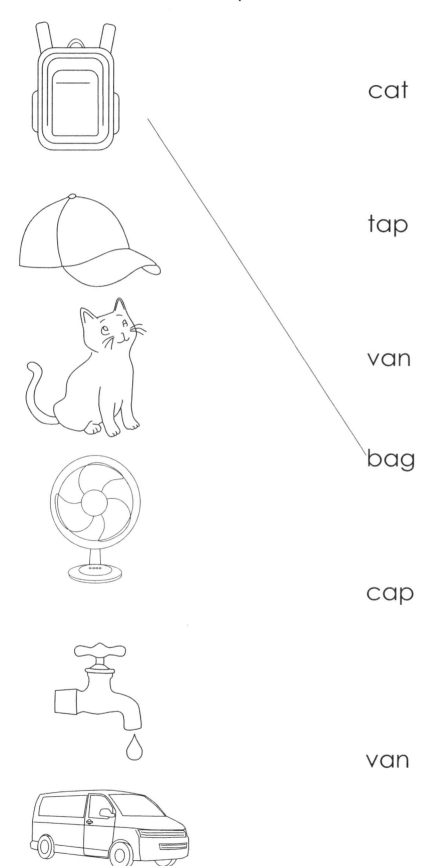

cat

tap

van

bag

cap

van

Date:_____Title:_____

Say the name of each object and write the missing sound.

☐ ag

☐ at

☐ an

☐ ap

☐ at

| c | m | t | f | c |

Date:_____Title:_____

Say the name of each object, sound and write it.

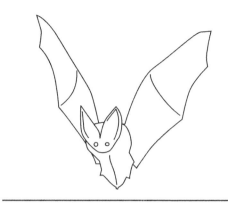

_____

....

_____

_____

....

_____

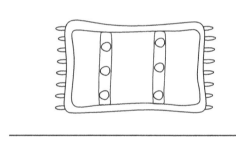

_____

....

_____

_____

....

_____

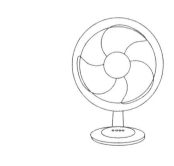

_____

....

_____

_____

....

_____

23

Date:_____Title:_____

Wordlist
Write 5 words with sound **a**

bag

rat

cap

tap

hat

_____

_____

_____

_____

_____

_____

_____

_____

_____

_____

Date:_____Title:_____

Dictation

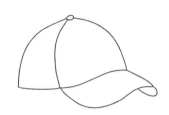

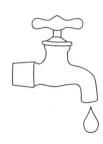

Sight words
Say and write each word four times.

I

to

do

we

the

he

she

me

was

Date:_____Title:_____

Read and re-write each sentence.

A fan

A van

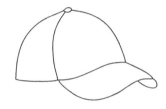

A cap

A cat

A bag

Box 2
Short Vowel 'e'

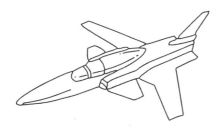

Date:_____Title:_____

Touch and say the name of each object and write the beginning sound.

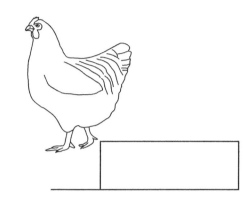

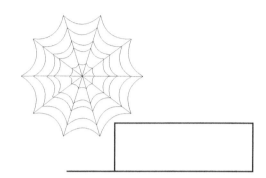

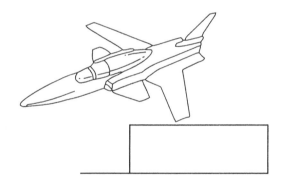

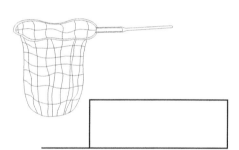

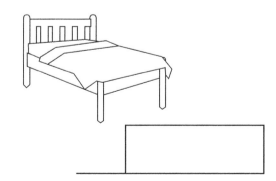

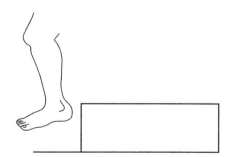

29

Date:_____Title:_____

Sound, blend and write

p + e + g =

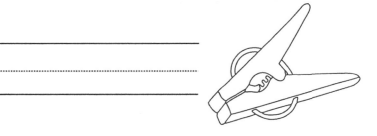

_____
- - - - - - - - - - - -
_____

n + e + t =

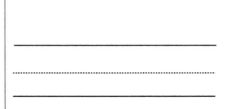

_____
- - - - - - - - - - - -
_____

h + e + n =

_____
- - - - - - - - - - - -
_____

l + e + g =

_____
- - - - - - - - - - - -
_____

w + e + b =

_____
- - - - - - - - - - - -
_____

b + e + d =

_____
- - - - - - - - - - - -
_____

30

Date:_____Title:_____

Match the picture with the correct word

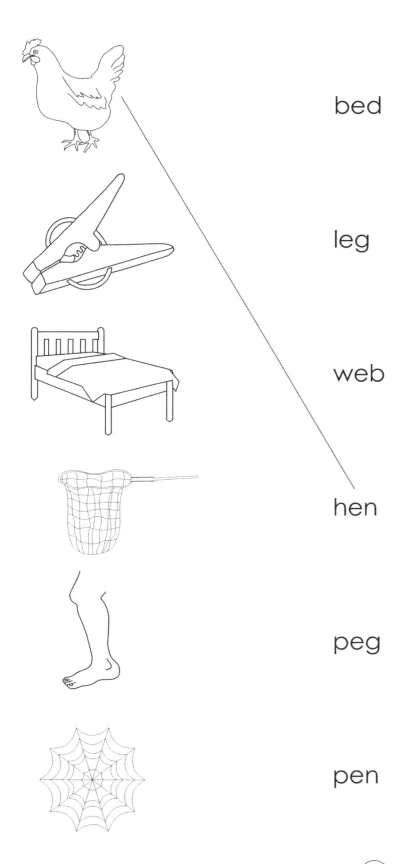

bed

leg

web

hen

peg

pen

Date:_____Title:_____

Word find
circle the word that matches the object

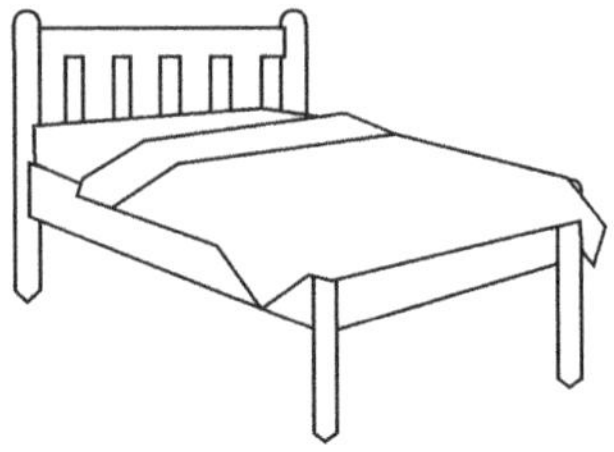	hen bed
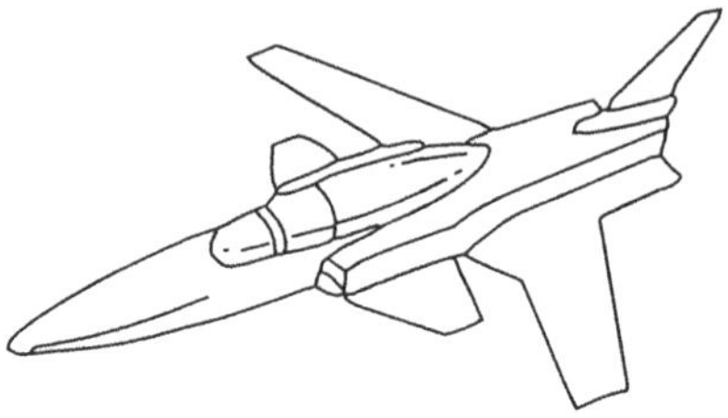	jet leg
	jam leg
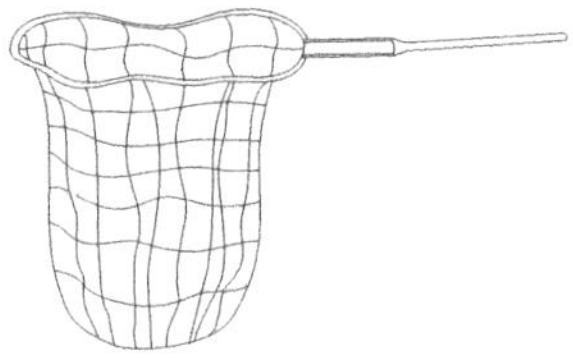	net mop
	bag hen

Date:_____Title:_____

Say the name of each object and circle the word that matches the object.

leg   mop

hat   bed

jet   leg

egg   web

cot   hen

peg   keg

Date:_____Title:_____

Wordlist
Write 5 words with sound e

bed
leg
jet
hen
net

_____

_____

_____

_____

_____

_____

Date:_____Title:_____

Dictation

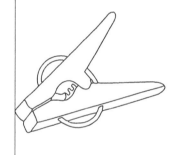

Date:_____Title:_____

Sight words
Say and write each word 4 times

be _____

all _____

do _____

we _____

are _____

he _____

she _____

you _____

was _____

Date:_____ Title:_____

Read and re-write each sentence.

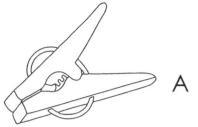 A peg

 A hen

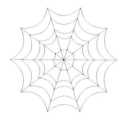 A web

 A leg

 A pen

Box 3
Short Vowel 'i'

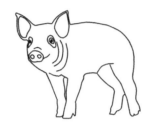

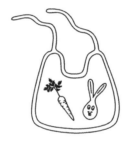

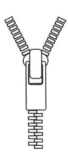

38

Date:_____Title:_____

Touch and say the name of each object and write the beginning sound.

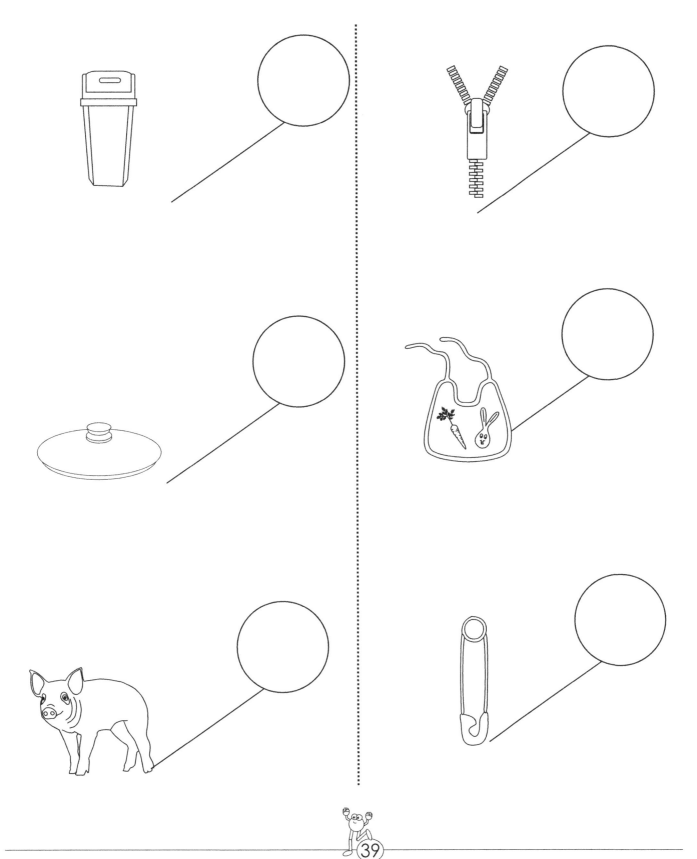

Date:_____Title:_____

Sound, blend and write

p + i + n = _____

t + i + n = _____

b + i + b = _____

z + i + p = _____

l + i + p = _____

l + i + d = _____

40

Date:_____Title:_____

Match the picture with the correct word

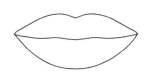

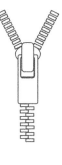

tin

pin

lid

bib

lip

zip

Date:_____Title:_____

Say the name of each object, sound and write it.

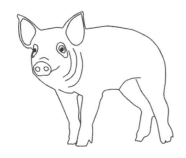

_____

....

_____

_____

....

_____

_____

....

_____

_____

....

_____

_____

....

_____

Wordlist
Write 5 words with sound i

hip
lid
tin
lit
lip

_____
....
_____
....
_____
....
_____
....
_____
....
_____
....
_____
....

Date:_____Title:_____

Dictation

Date:_____Title:_____

Sight words
Say and write each word 4 times

be _____

all _____

do _____

we _____

are _____

he _____

she _____

you _____

was _____

Date:_____Title:_____

Read and re-write each sentence.

A tin

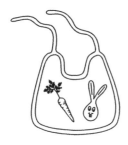

A bib

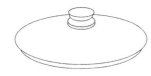

A lid

A pin

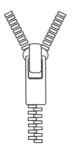

A zip

Box 4
Short Vowel 'o'

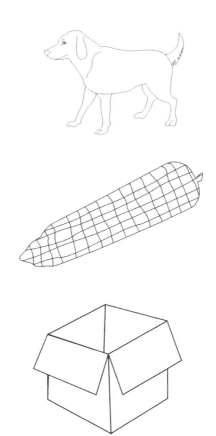

Date:_____ Title:_____

Touch and say the name of each object and write the beginning sound.

Date:_____Title:_____

Sound, blend and write

p + o + t =

_____
....
_____

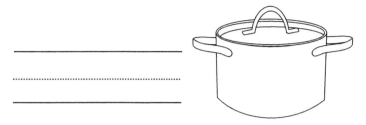

t + i + n =

_____
....
_____

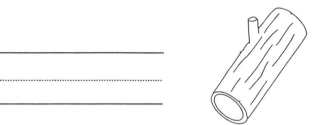

b + o + x =

_____
....
_____

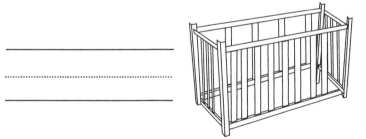

c + o + t =

_____
....
_____

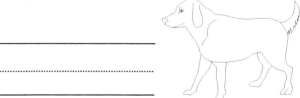

d + o + g =

_____
....
_____

Date:_____Title:_____

Say the name of each object and circle the word that matches the object.

 cot

mop

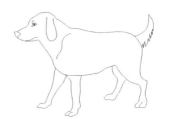 pot

dog

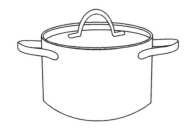 pot

cot

 mop

yam

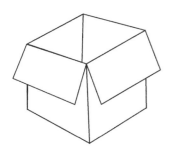 bag

box

 hen

log

Date:_____Title:_____

Say it, connect it and write it.

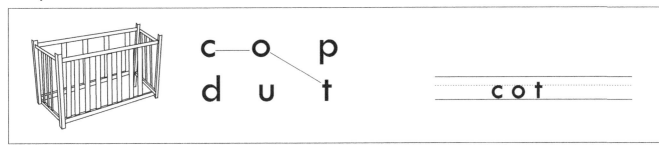

c — o   p
d   u   t

c o t

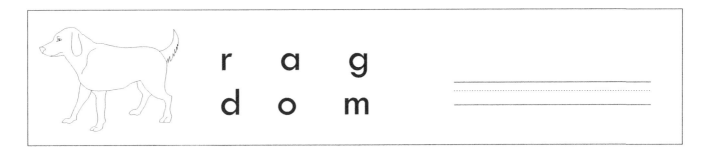

r   a   g
d   o   m

_____

p   l   n
l   o   t

_____

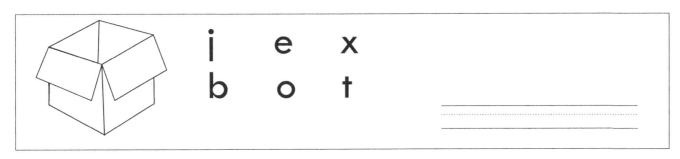

j   e   x
b   o   t

_____

k   e   g
l   o   m

_____

Date:_____ Title:_____

Say the name of each object, sound and write it.

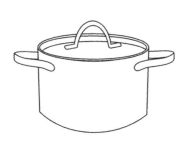

_____
- - - - - - - - - - - - - - - - -
_____

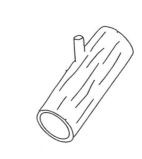

_____
- - - - - - - - - - - - - - - - -
_____

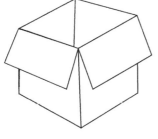

_____
- - - - - - - - - - - - - - - - -
_____

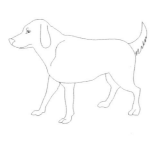

_____
- - - - - - - - - - - - - - - - -
_____

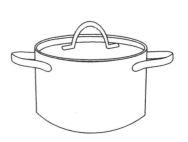

_____
- - - - - - - - - - - - - - - - -
_____

Date:_____Title:_____

Wordlist
Write 5 words with sound o

cot
pot
log
top

Date:_____ Title:_____

Dictation

Say the name	Sound and write the letters	Write the name
				....
				....
				....
			....
				....

Date:_____Title:_____

Sight words
Say and write each word 4 times

you _____

was _____

be _____

here _____

there _____

they _____

any _____

come _____

before _____

Date:_____Title:_____

Read and re-write each sentence.

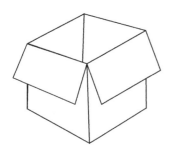 A box

 A pot

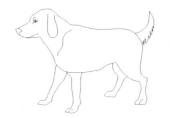 A dog

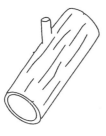 A log

 A mop

Box 5
Short Vowel 'u'

Date:_____Title:_____

Touch and say the name of each object

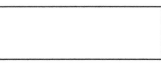

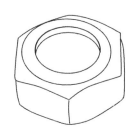

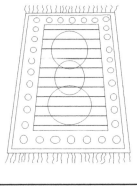

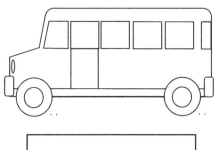

Date:_____Title:_____

Sound, blend and write

b + u + s =   _____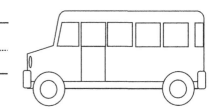

c + u + p =   _____

g + u + n =   _____

b + u + g =   _____

s + u + n =   _____

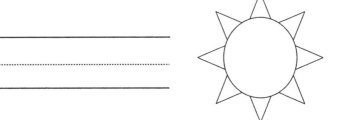

Date:_____Title:_____

Match the picture with the correct word

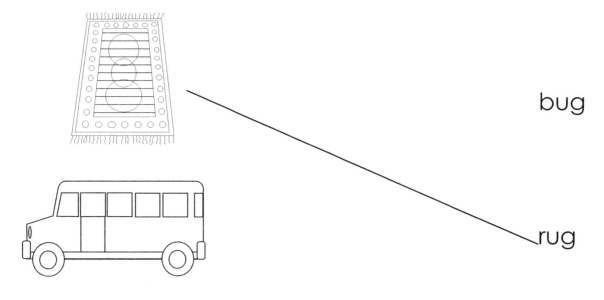

bug

rug

nut

sun

cup

bus

Date:_____Title:_____

Word find

circle the word that match the object

	cup	big
	van	bus
	tub	leg
	keg	jug
	nut	hen

Date:_____Title:_____

Say the name of each object, sound and write it.

_____
....
_____

_____
....
_____

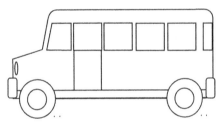

_____
....
_____

_____
....
_____

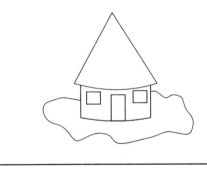

_____
....
_____

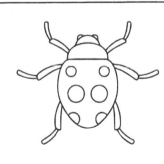

_____
....
_____

Date:_____Title:_____

Word list
Write 5 words with sound u

hut
nut
bug
mug

_____

_____

_____

_____

_____

_____

_____

_____

Dictation

Say the name	Sound and write the letters	Write the name

64

Sight words
Say and write each word 4 times

you

was

be

here

there

they

any

come

before

Date:_____Title:_____

Read and re-write each sentence.

A bus

A hut

A jug

A bug

A tub

Date:_____Title:_____

Sight words
Say and write each word 4 times

you _____

was _____

be _____

here _____

there _____

they _____

any _____

come _____

before _____

Date:_____Title:_____

Read and re-write each sentence.

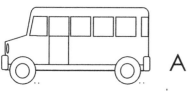 A bus

 A jug

 A hut

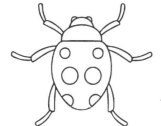 A bug

 A tub

Date:_____Title:_____

Identify each object and write the middle sound.

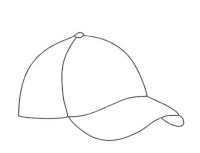

c __ p

b __ g

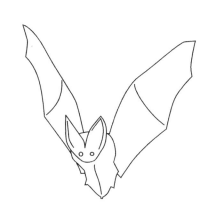

b ___ t

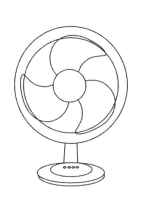

f ___ n

c___ t

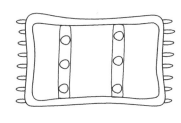

m___ t

h __ t

p___ n

v __ n

Identify each object and write the middle sound.

b__d	l__g	h___n
w__b	J__t	n__t
p__n		p__g

Date:_____Title:_____

Identify each object and write the middle sound.

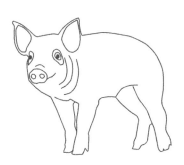

p____g

b____b

b____n

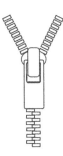

z____p

p____n

t____n

Date:_____Title:_____

Identify each object and write the middle sound.

p__t

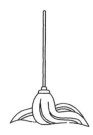

m__p

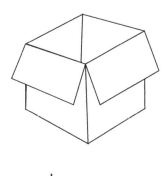

b__x

c__t

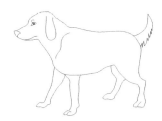

d__g

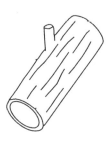

l__g

Date:_____Title:_____

Identify each object and write the middle sound.

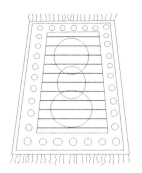

r__g

h __ t

j__g

b__s

n__t

s__n

Date:_____Title:_____

Identify each object and write the middle sound.

p__t

h__n

b__g

c__t

t__b

b__b

Date:_____Title:_____

Identify each object and match to the correct sentence

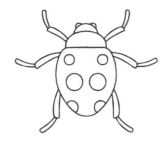

A red cap.

The fat cat is on a mat.

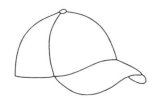

The hat and a cat.

A red bug.

A big pan.

Date:_____Title:_____

Read each sentence and complete with the name of each object.

A red _____

A fat _____

A big _____

Tom has a tan _____

A bug hid in the _____

She has a big _____

Date:_____Title:_____

Read each sentence and match to the correct object.

A fat dog.

A big jug.

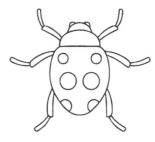

The sun is hot.

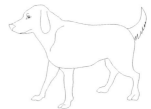

She has a big hat.

The red bug is big.

The pig is on a lid.

Date:_____Title:_____

Identify each object and write the name in sentence.

The big _____ is on a pot

A big _____

Tom has a tan _____

Ken has a red _____

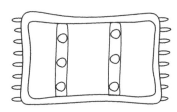

A bug hid in the _____

Date:_____Title:_____

Read and rewrite each sentence

The pen is in the bin

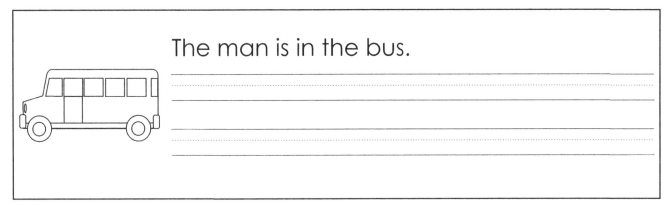

The man is in the bus.

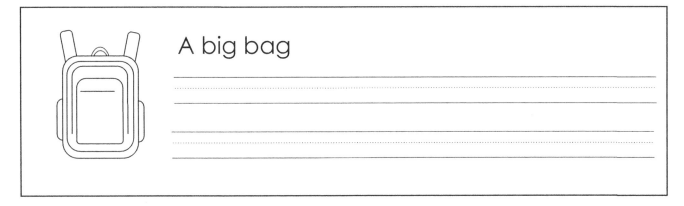

A big bag

A big fat dog

Date:_____ Title:_____

I can sort words with short "a", "e", "i", "o" and "u"

a

e

u

bag bug tin pot net rug cot lip mug dot fun cap fin hat
log jet sin mop mat kit ten map bin jug jot rat pin top
leg bat keg gun can hen pan beg run pig sun vet hot

Pink Wordlist

a	e	i
bat	beg	bin
ban	ben	bib
bag	get	did
cat	hen	dig
cap	jet	fin
can	keg	fig
dad	leg	fit
fan	met	hit
fat	men	kit
hat	net	kin
ham	pet	lip
lap	pen	lid
man	set	pin
map	ten	pig
nap	let	sit
pan	wet	tin
pat	web	vim
rat	bet	sin
ram	yet	sip
sat	let	sin

Pink Wordlist

o	u
cot	cut
dot	cup
got	bud
hot	bus
log	fun
mop	gun
rot	hut
pot	jug
son	mug
ton	nun
won	run
box	rug
mom	sun
	pud

Date:_____ Title:_____

Date:_____ Title:_____

Date:_____ Title:_____

Date:_____ Title:_____

_____
....
_____
....
_____

_____
....
_____

_____
....
_____

_____
....
_____

_____
....
_____

_____
....
_____

_____
....
_____

Date:_____Title:_____

Ogabidu O. Emmanuel © 2022

Date:_____ Title:_____

Date:_____ Title:_____

Made in the USA
Coppell, TX
07 September 2023

21306347R00052